CW01560345

SO YOU WANT TO BE A CONSULTANT

TIPS
FROM THE SECRET FILES OF THE PROFESSIONALS

AUTHOR NOTES:

JON WARNER has over 20 years experience in a number of major multi-national companies in the United Kingdom, Europe, the United States of America and Australia. This experience has included time as a senior staff manager in human resources and a number of line roles with responsibility for large groups of people. During the last 5 years Jon has been involved in broad ranging organisational consultancy and the pursuit of best-practice leadership. This consulting has taken him into a number of major organisations such as Mobil Oil, the National Bank, BTR, Qantas, Gas and Fuel, United Energy, Air Products and Chemicals , Honda and Pepsi-Cola. Jon is also Managing Director of Team Publications Pty Limited, an international training and publishing company committed to bringing practical and fun-to-use learning material to the training market.

PAUL ROBERTSON has been a senior professional manager with over 30 years experience in many multi-national companies in the United Kingdom, continental Europe and the United States of America. In the last twelve years, Paul has run a large and successful management consultancy, training and management learning resources business in the United Kingdom. This has brought him into contact with a wide range of diverse clients at all levels of the organisation.

JACK NEWNHAM is a professional cartoonist, working as a hired pencil for 25 odd years. Well ~ mostly odd, some were even. Cartoons are good for communicating information, so examples of his work litter the field of advertising, public relations and education. His working creed, based on actual results, is ~ 'a good cartoon is worth 348 words' (not counting swear words). That's why the authors asked him to contribute to this book ~ to save them the extra work.

SO YOU WANT TO BE A CONSULTANT

TIPS

**FROM THE SECRET FILES
OF THE PROFESSIONALS**

**Jon Warner, BA(Hons), MBA, CMAHRII, FBIM
Paul Robertson, BA(Hons), MBIM
Cartoons and illustrations by Jack Newnham**

Pearson Education Australia
Unit 4, Level 2
14 Aquatic Drive
Frenchs Forest NSW 2086

Publisher: Nella Soeterboek
Project Editor: Sarah Welling
Cover designed by Ramsay Macfarlane Design, NSW
Cartoonist: Jack Newnham

Printed in Australia by Griffin Press

1 2 3 4 5 04 03 02 01 00

National Library of Australia
Cataloguing-in-Publication data

Warner, Jonathon Charles.
So you want to be a consultant: tips from the secret files of the professionals.

ISBN 1 74009 433 6.

1. Consultants. 2. Consultants—Marketing. 3. Business Consultants.
I. Robertson, Paul. II. Title.

658.46

An imprint of Pearson Education Australia.

Contents

The loneliness of
the non-consulted consultant.

Introduction

Consultancy can be a lonely business, especially in the early days when the novelty of being your own boss gives way to the stark realisation that the only income you're going to get depends entirely on your own efforts ~ and that includes finding someone who's prepared to pay good money for your skills and talents...

'*So you wanna be a Consultant*' sets out to provide guidelines for the self-employed consultant, whether you're looking for help to get started or new ideas you can use to increase your existing business. It's written and compiled by consultants who have learnt from their own mistakes and successes in a variety of business sectors.

Overriding all the tips in this book are two major principles which every consultant must keep firmly in mind ~ one is an absolute dedication to your clients and their needs and interests and the other is the maintenance of the very highest level of professionalism in all of your dealings.

Part of that professionalism is efficient and effective marketing of yourself and your services. '*So you wanna be a consultant*' will help you to be a better marketer.

A moment of reflection before entering the fray …

This book gives practical tips, advice and guidance in four sections.

These are:

1. Actively marketing your services: Passive and Dynamic promotion

2. Charging for your services

3. Managing the client relationship

4. Maintaining and developing your consultancy

Each section merely serves as an 'umbrella' under which to categorise the tips. Although the book follows a logical path, feel free to 'dip' into it at any point as you wish.

Feel free to 'dip' in …

SECTION 1

Actively marketing your services

Tips on 'passive' and 'dynamic' promotion

Regular promotion activity is a must

You should be spending up to a quarter of your time every week marketing your services, especially when you are busy. If you wait until things are quiet, you'll be too late to fill the troughs with new business.

There are generally, two types of promotion, 'passive' and 'dynamic'.

You need both types to attract clients.

Part A gives tips on passive promotion.
Part B on dynamic promotion.

Passive promotion

Printed announcements, eg brochures, leaflets, letters, posters, signs, advertisements in journals and press, radio, television, Internet site, trade directories.

Passive promotion pieces reveal the scope and strengths of your consultancy with an invitation for prospective customers to make contact, usually by telephone, E-mail, fax or post. Passive promotion pieces are left at strategic sites or delivered directly to selected addresses where, hopefully, they will be snatched up by prospects who will gleefully respond and come panting to your door.

Dynamic promotion

Where you, personally, go 'prospecting' for customers. You can 'prospect' in a variety of ways including –

(i)   Arrange to meet carefully selected or other prospective client decision-makers and persuade them to hire your services.

(ii) Make presentations at business gatherings where you will be seen by many influential people.

(iii) Contribute articles and letters to the most important press media in your field of business. Eventually you can build a reputation as a consultant with 'desirable', 'informed' and out of the ordinary management skills

PART A:
Passive Promotion.
Where you sit back and hope the patron saint
of consultancy smiles on you.

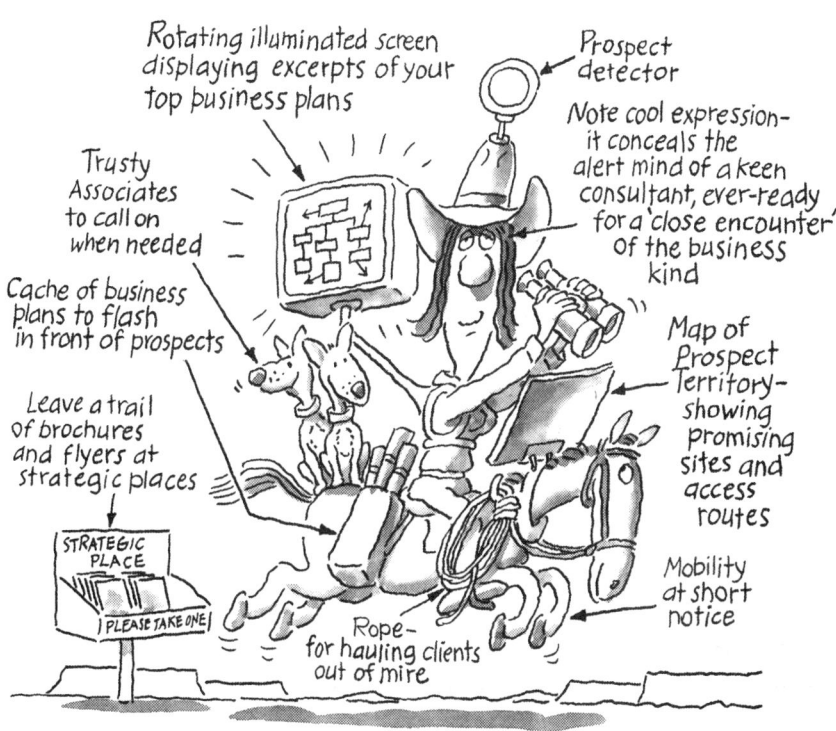

PART B:
Dynamic Promotion.

Riding the promotional trail, where you
actively prospect for clients by:
- Sewing a few seeds in fertile soil
- Making a few waves
- Pitching a few proposals
- Dealing a few wild cards and generally.....................

.... pulling your finger out!

Part A: Passive promotion tips

You'll need more than a CV or resume to attract business

You'll probably need to write a CV or resume for some clients files, but CV's rarely work very well as an up-front marketing piece. Where they do work is where they accidentally describe a job or assignment that is similar to the work that currently interests a particular client.

"One human resource consultant has 8 versions of their resume. Each is printed on different coloured paper and emphasises a particular aspect of the consultant's experience or skill. This is used as an attachment to a prospecting letter or insert to their brochure."

Your business card ~ not a full blown directory

Try not to use your business card like a poster site advertising all your wares. This not only gives the impression that you're a jack of all trades but also selects out people who might have been interested in contacting you.

"The record number of words (so far!), on the back of a business card is 37! This included the consultant's vision, mission and values in font so small that you almost needed a magnifying glass to read it."

Poor quality promotional material
can be a liability ~ an opportunity lost …

Excellent high quality promotional material will work for you

Your printed promotion material should reflect the high standard of your consulting work. As a general guide, the quality should match the quality of the material your prospects see in their marketplace. Modern technology has lifted the overall standard substantially ~ second or third generation photocopied promotional material just isn't going to 'cut it' these days. Good quality paper and printing are a plus, but all your promotion has this primary aim ~ to communicate clearly what a valuable resource you are.

"For over 12 months, a new consultant was using a laser printed sheet of paper to describe her services. Because she didn't keep the original, and only printed a few copies at a time, by the end of the 12 months, some paragraphs in fourth and fifth generation photocopies were barely visible. Client secretaries started telling her to please send better copies!"

Your sales pitch in print ~ what to emphasise

If you do produce a brochure or sales piece, don't make it too long or comprehensive. If you tell the whole story, your prospects may not need to get in touch with you. Better to establish what you can do so that prospects can identify areas where you can help them. An eight to ten point bulleted list of your areas of expertise is often a good approach.

"Large management consultancies often insist that a particular 'sales pitch' in print is restricted to one page with 5 or 6 bullet points describing how this can specifically add value to a client organisation. They reason that a client will normally only spend 20 to 30 seconds in reading any sales pitch in writing."

Direct mail promotion ~ brochures, newsletters, etc...

If you want to use direct mail, use it to reinforce your relationships with existing clients, it rarely works when sent to cold lists. By all means test cold list mailings in very small quantities, and if they do work ~ carry on! If not, ask yourself which approaches have worked best for you in the past and develop these. It is also important to always use people's name and job titles in your meetings and not 'The Human Resource Manager'.

"A small financial consultancy firm uses direct mail to inform its client base about new services and about its capability to handle assignments when change occurs (new tax laws etc). This single page letter has now grown to become a quarterly newsletter that many of the client base eagerly awaits. The firm estimates that this newsletter now generates over 50% of new work for them."

Servicing more than one market sector

If you service more than one target market, write a separate brochure for each one and concentrate on the benefits you can offer to each type of client. A general brochure selling all your services is not usually specific enough to stimulate response.

"The longest consultant services brochure (so far!) runs to 64 colour pages describing almost every industrial sector under the sun. Client feedback suggested that it successfully communicated that this consulting business was large, diverse, and obviously highly skilled. However, it also suggested big expensive overheads, lack of focus and lack of relevance to particular clients ~ they stopped using it!"

This studio portrait proved to be a very
successful ice breaker at client meetings.

... when it could have been s-o-o-o different!

Invest in a good portrait photo

If you do use a photograph of yourself in your publicity material, get a professional photographer who specialises in business portraiture. A scruffy Polaroid with you shown with a plant growing out of your head in your front room will do more harm than good!

"A relatively young (and he would say good looking consultant) put his photo on his business card. When he turns up for client meetings, his card is often a great 'ice breaker' as they talk about how good studio shots can be."

Make it easy for prospects to respond

If you use direct mail, you can lift response considerably by including a reply device to enable prospects to respond to you easily, such as a card or business reply envelope and coupon. This also means that you can control the information you want them to send you.

"One small consultant uses a diagonal triangle at the bottom right of her single page promotional letter every time she sends them out. This allows people to write their name, job title, area of greatest focus, before sending back the cut off triangle in a pre-paid envelope. They do this in response to a special offer, competition, to obtain free information, etc... On average, this consultant gets a remarkable 15% of her mailing total to respond directly."

Is your promotional copy readable?
If you don't have one at your house, try to borrow a
12 or 13 year old to act as a 'waffle' detector.

The business letter ~ your chance to talk at length

Don't be afraid of using a long copy in business letters or leaflets. Provided that what you have to say is interesting and relevant to your reader, long copy will generally outperform short copy. Try to make your writing as relevant to the particular client as possible ~ even a quick bit of research on the telephone first can give you some very useful clues.

"One particular client complained as follows ~ 'I am tired of large consulting organisations just dropping in any company's name to replace the last one that they wrote to. These days, if they don't trouble to find out a bit more about us and include it in their letter and proposals, I will just not use them'."

Preparing your promotional copy (text)

Make your promotional copy clear and easy to read using 'every day' words. Any selling copy that you write should be readily understandable and readable. Test it out on a 12 or 13 year old then ask them to tell you what they think you have said. Any copy that exceeds the reading level of the average popular newspaper just won't get read ~ and you won't get the business.

"One consulting organisation makes sure that copy text going to a client is read first by another consultant in the business. Their job is to look for long words, confusing concepts, jargon and acronyms ~ these are cut out or re-written."

Closet rap!

Test your communication ideas before production

When it comes to writing marketing communications, once again, it is wise to test it out on people (including your family members) and ask them what their perception is of the person that wrote it and the product offered. It's best to pick people who don't care too much about hurting your feelings!

"One sole operator consultant likes to use his family to test out brochures, leaflets and letters. If his wife and 2 teenage daughters don't understand a word or a concept he changes the copy so that they will ~ he encourages direct feedback and now often gets it straight from the shoulder."

Read it aloud ~ does it flow and make sense?

As a general tip for writing copy, read out aloud what you have written, and if it sounds awkward, change it. We tend to read to ourselves anyway because of the way we were taught to read at school. However, copy that doesn't flow when read aloud, can be clumsy and hard to read for a client.

"One consultant not only reads their letters aloud but with as much verbal feeling and emphasis as possible ~ his favourite place to do this is in the toilet!"

Personalising business correspondence

Direct marketing specialists have found that a handwritten PS on a letter substantially increases the impact of the letter and will make it stand out. However, the PS needs to be a point of real added value like "If you would like a free full copy of my article on this topic please call".

"A large corporate executive said that he likes to read a post script first (if there is one) to see if there is something of interest, before reading the rest of the letter."

A 'tease' device to awaken interest

One way of using the PS is to give enough information to intrigue the reader but not enough to tell the whole story, so that readers have to read the body copy of your letter, eg "You may not believe it but it really was the best I'd ever seen!"

"One of the best post script teasers to a letter (so far!) was ~ 'PS . We ended up saving our last client well over a million with 4 simple strategies'."

The fateful ad

YES! It's THAT ad!

The Professional Journal.
Where wandering professionals reveal their deepest needs.

Use the trade press and directories to advertise your wares

Someone out there needs you ~ keep your name up front. Make sure you have some kind of entry in the trade and professional directories, however small, relevant to your market sector ~ many offer free or low cost entries, so the investment needn't be huge. You don't need full page, four colour advertisements but you should exploit the opportunity for prospect companies to find you.

"Contrary to the belief of small consulting organisations or single operators, large consultants make sure that they are listed in as many directories and in professional magazines everywhere ~ they believe that advertising is responsible for as much as 25% of new business by keeping their name top of mind."

Have information readily available on request

Try producing an information 'product' relevant to your area of expertise that your prospects can request from you as part of your advertising thrust. This establishes your knowledge credibility and allows you to pre-screen leads.

"One consulting firm has created over 25 information 'products'. They are simple checklists of 'do's' and 'don'ts' relevant to the industry they serve. These checklists were based on post-consulting experience and have the function of demonstrating the firms aptitude and credibility for new clients, as well as giving useful information."

Value-added extras featured in your advertising
could give you an edge.

Charge a small fee

Test charging a nominal fee for your information product. This will often give you better leads and prospects who won't spend a little more on useful information are unlikely to pay for your services anyway.

"The same consulting firm now promotes its checklists as a small money generating device. Checklists are offered for a nominal price and are delivered personally so that the implementation strategy can be discussed."

If you call before 30th June you get a prize!

Use some form of 'earlybird' device to overcome your prospects natural inertia ~ even if they are interested they tend to leave things to the last minute or may even forget about you altogether. By offering an extra benefit or advantage for responding before a given date, you will increase your chances of getting response and starting the relationship.

"One consulting firm uses many natural deadlines like year end, summer holidays, Christmas, Easter, etc, to offer special prices or an extra service if the response beats the deadline."

The 'Flamboyant Spectacle'.
(Attention grabber ~ lacks credibility).
Where you plan an 'event', and invite prospects to observe your ability
to manipulate management factors with ease and style.

Part B: Dynamic promotion tips

The more dynamic side of actively marketing your services simply involves being "out there". The shy and quiet consultant who hopes that their reputation for excellence will be sufficient to see clients beating a path to their door, is either very famous (for past efforts or other achievements) or soon to be very short of work!

Your a great consultant ~ get out there and show them!

Speaking at public forums.
Don't forget to bring your sense of humour,
(along with your sense of taste and proportion).

Building your image as an authority in your field

You should be spending about half of the time you've put aside for marketing on building your reputation and image as a source of knowledge in your chosen field. You can do this by appearing on public platforms, writing articles and becoming a recognised force in your professional or trade associations. Consider talk-back radio interviews and an internet site.

Speaking at public forums ~ an opportunity to meet prospects

If you do get onto public platforms don't simply leave copies of your marketing material lying around in the hope that delegates will pick one up. It's far more effective to mention during your session that you have an informative and useful product and that you'll be pleased to send a copy to delegates who hand you a business card. This gives you an excellent mailing list and the cluster of people talking to you after your speech will enhance your reputation with the organisers of the session!

"One popular consultant on the public speaking 'circuit' organises himself to collect business cards in a glass bowl on the promise that he guarantees to get back to each person either on the telephone or in writing to discuss how his presentation applies to the person's own situation ~ he regularly collects 10-15% of the audience business cards every time he speaks."

Client gatherings.
Impress several clients or prospects at one time.
Invite them to meet and discuss subjects of mutual interest which
could influence their future planning.

Client gatherings ~ invitations to discuss the latest market developments

A good way to impress several clients or prospects at a time is to hold regular meetings ~ say, four to six times a year ~ to discuss a topic relevant to all. Topics could be "The Implications of the new multi-media technology" or "Using Market Research to Increase Profits", and the discussion should be led by you, so giving you the chance to identify potential client needs and demonstrate your own expertise at the same time.

"A two-person consulting business likes to scan the professional journals and magazines to identify major topics of interest in order to pick a topic that is likely to stimulate interest at their next quarterly breakfast seminar. These events are regular and popular gatherings and always create leads and opportunities in new and often different types of consulting."

Prepare introduction and closing notes

You will help yourself and your host at conferences or seminars by preparing a short written introduction and closing note so that it can be used to 'top and tail' your presentation.

"An experienced consultant who speaks publicly on a regular basis advises that it is wise to carry cards in your pocket that have short typed summary introduction and closing remarks. He says he has lost count of the times that he has pulled out the cards to calm his nerves as he opens his talk and ensures that the close is strong and confident."

The Great Overhead Projector Disaster of '99!

Presentations at fairs, conferences, seminars ~ doing your party piece

You can add to your industry and general profile by putting together two or three short presentations on relevant topics which can be offered to groups or conference organisers on occasions where your prospects are likely to be in attendance. Organisers are always on the look out for good speakers and should welcome such approaches. If you're not a good speaker, invest in training yourself to become more proficient.

"A small consulting firm collected all the flyers and leaflets that they received individually and as a business. This showed them that only 7 or 8 companies were involved in organising 90% of the conferences and seminars. They then wrote and spoke to each of the conference organisers to offer to speak ~ over the next 12 months they spoke at 3 conferences and 2 seminars and significantly increased market awareness of their firm."

Always check and test mechanical and electronic equipment

Always check the physical 'props' well before making a speech or presentation. Check the projector, the microphone, the screen, the lectern or whatever before you get introduced ~ because once you're on, it's too late!

"Even the best kind of plans can trip you up! One consultant tripped over the overhead projector cord and broke the machine, blew the projector bulb in the back up machine and was left talking to the audience in his loudest voice because of feedback problems when trying to use the microphone!"

The 'Mutual Benefit Courtship'.
Your aim: Persuade the prospect that you were made for each other ~
(faint heart ne'r won fat fee).

Tips for interviewing prospects

Courting a prospect

It's never easy to win business from cold calls, especially if you appear to need the business. Far better to make an appointment to see a prospect about an article or a paper you are writing and seek their advice or input. Make sure that you send them a copy of the finished work of course! During the interview you will have plenty of opportunities to talk about what you do and how it could meet the needs of the prospect.

"A small, independent sales and marketing consultant likes to ring sales and marketing managers in large companies to obtain 'research data' as input for something they are writing or researching. They claim that 95% of people like to feel their opinion is worthwhile to a consultant and will jump at the chance to talk about themselves or their business ~ this is a great platform to build upon."

Who to contact

Your promotional efforts should be directed at the manager or executive in a prospect company who can make the decisions in your area of skill or potential contribution. Don't go through the Personnel or Human Resource manager unless, of course, this is your target department.

"One consulting firm has a policy of avoiding intermediaries of all sorts and aims to talk to divisional heads, or executive line managers only. Even when they end up working with the intermediaries or more junior staff they only do this knowing they have the authority and support of the executive."

...I'm a business consultant currently researching a NOVEL about the conflicts and shifting fortunes of people in today's corporate world. I'd really LOVE some AUTHENTIC IN-PUT from a REAL-LIFE manager, fearlessly making decisions at the CUTTING EDGE, like yourself... We could maybe set up a meeting where you interview me as an outside consultant who, in my story, saves your business from impending ruin and then...

Manouvering for an interview.
Doing 'Creative Research'
How creative can you get?
Turns out she didn't get a second interview,
but the book was a best seller.

Arranging appointments ~ an exercise in professionalism

Under no circumstances should you grovel! Clients don't like to do business with people who are overly eager to please. When you're setting a meeting date, for example, don't say "anytime tomorrow will be fine", but say "I can be available next Wednesday from 9.00 to 11.00 a.m. ~ would this suit you?"

"Staring at several blank pages in your diary can be demotivating. One consultant enters all the activities of the week (business and home) to fill up a few areas. This allows her to genuinely tell prospective clients that she has a meeting at 2pm next Wednesday but she can meet after 3pm (the 2pm meeting may only be going to the bank!)."

What to wear

Try to dress in the same manner as your clients or prospects, within reason-i.e. not excessively formal or informal. If in doubt, err on the side of formality. In all circumstances aim to be smart and neat ~ scruffy is a 'look' that very few can get away with.

"One consultant has a range of ties to suit every occasion. He uses dark and conservative ties for engineering and technical clients and bright light and even comic ties for technology and retail clients."

Preamble of a 'laid-back waffle-duck'.
Smooth on the surface, paddling hard below.

Prospecting ~ play it cool

Even if you are 'gasping' for business, try not to seem desperate. You will appear more of a 'catch' if clients assume your air of slight indifference means that they need you more than you need them. Of course 'cool' means calm and assured, not so aloof that they are wondering why you're there at all.

"Although we are often taught not to boast or brag, a large consulting organisation advises it's consulting staff to always name drop the clients they are currently working with. They believe this always helps credibility and sends a message that they are busy and in demand."

References? No sweat!

If you are asked for references, don't panic and go pale ~ you'll look inexperienced and your credibility will vanish. Be sufficiently prepared so that you can reach calmly into your briefcase and pull out a list (the longer the better). These don't have to be actual clients, but could include other business associates who can testify to your skills and talents. However, if you can ask past clients to give you references, so much the better.

"Just before becoming a consultant, one individual asked for, and obtained, several letters from customers attesting to their skills, professionalism and dependability. These references are still used with clients and regularly impress."

The 'Huff and Puff' approach.
Not recommended... unless the chief happens to be a
(a) hopeless or (b) your dad.

Talk to the 'chiefs' not the 'warriors'

Don't be cautious about insisting that you deal with decision makers. Dealing with intermediaries can be a waste of time and there is a good chance that your ideas and proposals may not be transmitted properly to the people that matter. (Don't be afraid to go to a higher level if necessary ~ sometimes you only get one chance to make your pitch).

"A highly successful lone consultant spends as much time on the telephone as she needs to in researching who a decision maker might be (working with reception, secretaries, etc...) before making her 'pitch' or organising a face-to-face interview. She believes this short time investment saves time in the long term."

Know which people are the chiefs?

If you're involved in 'selling' to a committee, talk to each individual who will be involved in the final decision beforehand and find out what their specific needs are within the greater picture. Show them how you can answer their individual needs, then, when you are in committee, demonstrate how you can provide the balance to ensure all the individual needs are met.

*"A partner in a very large international management consultancy suggests that most individual consultants are not concerned enough about the ultimate decision maker(s). In their view, a few simple questions about **who** this will be and what criteria will be used in the decision can reveal critical information that can help to re-shape your offering."*

Make the most of your interview.
This is your chance to 'ferret' out the vital
information, around which you make your 'pitch'.

Presenting to a board ~ get on the Agenda

If your business depends on the agreement of a board or executive team meeting, then try to get an invitation to attend the relevant meeting. Your best route is to convince the individual you deal with to get you onto the agenda and present during the discussion. This way you are available to answer any points and to sell yourself directly rather than relying on someone else to present your case.

"A very successful marketing consultant ensures that she asks the question about whether or not a decision has to be referred to a board or executive meeting at the outset. She advises that it is critical to know how your proposal will be presented, by whom and when. You don't always need to be in the room but by understanding the process you influence the result positively one more often than not."

Are you interviewing the client or being interviewed ~there's a big difference

Your client should realise that your time is valuable, if not more so, than theirs. You'll get more business by gaining the respect that comes from being busy and in demand and you can do this by controlling your early meetings with them and interviewing them rather than vice versa. This includes asking questions that give you the key data that helps to tailor your consulting offering.

"A strategic planning consulting business has developed a list of 20 key questions to ask a client at a first meeting if possible. Each question is written to be probing and direct ~ one example is 'what specific changes would you want to see in your workplace in one year from now?'"

The consultant who fell from Earth.

The five key questions

When you meet a prospect, be ready with the answers to the five questions that they never ask but still need answers for:

- How will I **benefit** from your services?
- Why will I **benefit** from working with you in particular?
- How can you prove that I will **benefit**?
- How much will I **benefit** from your advice?
- When will I see these **benefits**?

In every case, you need to be explicit ~ if you 'hedge' or talk in platitudes, you are unlikely to win the work.

"A small change-management consulting business likes to leave a simple piece of paper with its new clients after a first meeting ~ This paper is headed 'The benefits of working with us!'"

Questions say something about your competence

Don't waste your prospect's time by asking them questions you already know the answers to. It can make you seem bored and uninterested. If you've got nothing new or exciting or different to say, perhaps you shouldn't be talking to them at that time. Remember that each question should intelligently seek out responses that can help you to offer a product or a service that helps to add value to the client.

"One financial services consultant likes to prepare three questions before a meeting with a new prospect that will 'tease out' where the greatest added value to the client is likely to be. They write these questions down and aim to weave them into the conversation at a relevant point."

Allow me to begin our meeting
by reading from my MISSION STATEMENT...

" First off, please understand – I'm a
PROFESSIONAL, called to the practice
of Enterprise Consultancy.
During this interview I will require some straight-
forward answers to straight-forward questions.
I have no wish to WASTE OUR TIME by beating
about the bush, confusing issues or muddying
waters. The PROFESSIONAL approach is to be
forthright, direct and REAL, addressing
REAL PROBLEMS, coming up with REAL
solutions. Not pulling punches or ducking
the hard decisions. The road ahead leads
straight to the POINT. .We must avoid
pointless DETOURS along the way,
making REAL choices,
confronting the REAL nitty
gritty facts, coming
up with a REAL
no-nonsense agenda,
getting a REAL grasp
on the REAL issues,
getting REALLY REALLY
REALLY REAL..."

Unreal!!

Boring ~ boring ~ boring.

When to talk! When to listen!

When you're in a sales situation don't talk too much and don't try to be smart. The key selling skill in consulting is listening, not talking and you should only be talking for an absolute maximum of 40% of the time, preferably less. It's also a good idea to know what you're talking about but not to come across as a lot more intelligent than your client ~ you don't have to be the smartest person in the room to win work!

"Perhaps one of the largest consulting organisations in the world coaches its consultants to "dumb it down as much as possible". By this they aim to keep the explanations simple and the discussion clarification-oriented rather than to present lots of sophisticated ideas."

Watch your mouth ~ don't show all your cards

You will have to communicate to the client how you propose to tackle the job in hand, but don't be too detailed or the client may decide to do it without your help! Even worse, some clients actually set out to glean ideas from one or more consultants in order to give them enough clues to do the job for themselves!

"Many large consultants are often aware that some organisations will call for ideas, proposals and even detailed tenders in order to obtain suggestions that can be taken up without having to pay for the advice. As such, they are careful to describe what they are capable of doing and include just enough to elicit interest but not enough to see how a result might be achieved."

The lunch invitation ~ an approach that needs tact

You can embarrass a prospect by inviting them to lunch if they get the impression that they are going to be 'sold'. It's better to ask them out to give you advice on a particular issue where you know they have the expertise, then allow the conversation to turn inevitably and inexorably around to the services you provide and the how these can meet the client's needs.

"One human resource consultant aims to have 'lunch' once a week with a client or prospective client. They never look to sell any consulting services but use the meeting to ask what is happening in the client's industry and what problems or issues are upcoming. Clients are happy to oblige and often feel they are gaining a useful external perspective on issues they want to raise."

Doing Lunch

When a Prospect accepts an invitation from a Consultant to 'do' lunch an automatic agreement between the 'lunchees' is activated. It takes the form of a game, with agreed rules, so that proposals and counter proposals can proceed smoothly within the lunch format.

So! Players ready! Proposals ready! Waiters ready!

Let's play 'Lunchball'!

Rules for Lunchball

The Players: The Consultant (Pitcher), The Prospect (Receiver)

Pitching: The Pitcher is free to pitch a proposal to the Receiver at any time during the lunch. The Pitcher is bound to accept a refusal or non-committal response from the Receiver in good humour.

Receiving: The Receiver must consent to listen to the pitch respectfully with no sign of ridicule or mirth. The Receiver is free to accept, encourage, reject or be non-committal in response to the pitch.

It is acceptable, and makes the game more interesting, if the Receiver pitches a return proposal to encourage negotiations, where both players pitch and receive respectively.

If no pitch is accepted ~ no one wins the game.

If a pitch is accepted ~ both players win ~ celebrations all 'round.

The Pitcher pays for the lunch, unless it was the Receiver who issued the invitation to start the ball rolling in the first place. But that's another ball game.

Make your clients feel they get special attention.
Do you have a sympathetic desk-side manner? It could help you
to gain insight into the client's unique circumstances.

Attention to detail ~
make your clients feel they get special attention

Every client believes that their problem is unique and you should reinforce that impression. If you appear over-familiar with a given situation, you will make your clients think you are offering an 'off the shelf' solution, rather than applying your skills to their particular circumstances. Even if you have handled their particular problem hundreds of times before, it should appear 'fresh minted' ~ rather like the actor doing his one thousandth performance of Hamlet!

"Even the biggest consulting firms forget what makes the client feel unique sometimes ~ one large consulting business made a presentation to the Government about handling a very large contract over many months. They thought they had done a great job until one of the client team pointed out that they had the Government of another country in the header of their hand-out document. Needless to say, they did not feel very special and the consultants didn't get the work!"

Briefing the prospect ~
the part they play in the action

Make sure your prospects know exactly what action you want them to take at a given stage in the process; if necessary or relevant, spell out the stages in the relationship where the next action depends on them. This includes 'assumptive' closing conversations such as "so, by a week on Friday, you'll have sent me a full written brief ~ is that right?"

"A very large engineering consultancy often uses the strategy of putting the onus on the client to act ~ one way they do this is to suggest 'unless I hear from you to the contrary, I am happy to start work on this two weeks from today'."

The 'Hooray Henry Ambush'.
(calls for high energy and big white teeth).

Set realistic objectives ~ don't sell 'pie in the sky'

Don't oversell yourself. Make sure your clients know exactly what you can do and the probability that it will achieve the objectives set. However, make sure that they know what the risks are as well. Remember the old adage "under-promise and over-deliver." The majority of consultants do the reverse and get into trouble later.

"One large consulting practice always likes to add a day or two of extra time to complete a job, point to a few internal challenges to overcome and even occasionally suggest expenses that are a little higher than they might be. This is all part of their 'under promising' strategy which allows them to overcome their 'internal' challenges, finish the work a little earlier and submit slightly less in expenses."

Find out if the prospect is serious about using your services

You can pre-screen or 'qualify' your prospects simply by asking them if they are in a position to make a commitment to you, provided that you can demonstrate your ability to come up with a cost-effective method for solving their problem or help them to exploit a business opportunity. Its amazing how often this direct approach works-give it a try!

"A long established independent consultant advises that they ask for a commitment from a client at the second meeting at latest, wherever possible ~ they believe that for every client who says no, one says yes and they save significantly on extra wasted 'introductory' discussions."

... Calm and peaceful...
perfectly relaxed...
deeper and deeper...
deeply relaxed...
confident...
really confident now...
confident about the proposal...
you want to sign the authorisation...
for the consultant to begin the project...
NOW... RIGHT NOW...
you have great faith and confidence
in the consultant... no more DELAYS...
you WANT to sign...
NOW...

Er... um...
Yes...
I want to sign...
I CAN sign...
I WILL SIGN...
er... I think...

Delayed action.
Doubts, diversions and dawdlings. When the prospect presses
'freeze frame' and won't/can't push 'fast forward'!

Some prospects may need you to make the decision for them

If you find that prospects keep coming back to you for references or questions before they make the decision to take you on, it's likely that you aren't being sufficiently assertive or directive.

"Experienced consultants know that many clients can seemingly take forever to make a decision ~ a common strategy is to directly draw a conversation to a close by asking what it will take before a decision can be made. If this doesn't do the trick, the 'assumptive' close again is used."

Look at it this way ~ you'll look good, feel good and be nicer to your dog

If you find that prospects are still unsure of the wisdom of hiring you, don't forget to appeal to their emotion as well as their reason. Too often, we think that logic and reason are the only business appeals and forget that prospects are human too! Try to find ways that your services will benefit the prospect as a person ~ such as saving them time or enhancing their status within the organisation.

"One small consultancy always tries to find out as much as possible about the style, character and personal preferences of their prospective clients. This helps them to point out the advantages that will most appeal to a particular client, depending upon what is most important to them."

Professional etiquette ~ resist gossiping

Never discuss one client with another. You can, by all means, talk about past successes and even general non-attributable stories that are 'non-judgmental'. However, if you talk to a prospect about sensitive information from another client now, they'll assume that they'll be the ones to be discussed in the future.

"One management consultant was amazed to discover that they were developing a reputation as being 'indiscreet'. Upon investigation he discovered that what he saw as good stories about past clients to demonstrate his expertise, were being perceived as unnecessary gossip that might include them in the future ~ he quickly changed his habit."

Etiquette pays off ~ discuss your strengths not competitors failings

Don't knock or criticise your competition, or other consultants you know, in front of clients (even if the criticism might be justified). Be positive about what you can offer, concentrating on what you have that is unique in meeting clients' needs. If you are better, it will be apparent to your clients and prospects.

"A large manufacturing company executive likes to ask consultants what they think of other consulting firms or individuals. Whilst he always listens politely, he deliberately uses this conversation and the response elicited to test the consultant's overall integrity and capacity to resist the temptation to criticise."

The 'Tactical Retreat'.
When they fail to respond to your proposal, resist the temptation
to reveal their lack of good judgement!

Consultants ~ who needs them?

Some prospects will have reservations about working with a consultant, so try to tease out these fears in your initial contacts, discuss them and lay them to rest. This isn't easy, but if you sense any reluctance it is better not to ignore the issue ~ try asking such a client "You seem to be uncomfortable ~ can we talk about why this might be the case?"

"One consultant offers a simple approach for dealing with client trepidation about consultants. They spend a few minutes talking about their own concerns about common consultant shortfalls when they were in a similar position to their client. On most occasions this creates a common bond and helps to break any ice that might exist."

The non-compatible prospect
~ thanks but no thanks

When you find yourself faced with a prospect who doesn't really value you or your services, or who you feel has a personality type that will clash with yours, be bold and turn down the business. It could cost you dear in the long run in both frustration and emotional energy. One of the joys of consulting is being independent ~ this means you can ultimately choose who you'd like, and not like, to work with.

"An independent consultant specialising in executive counselling tells his clients that he may decline to take on the work after the initial 30 minute meeting. Although it happens rarely, he openly promotes the fact that he turns down around 5% of his clients offers of work to show that he is committed to a quality relationship that works for both parties."

The 'Desktop Tango'.
When the answer is "NO" but you're hearing "Maybe!"
Don't give up ~ many prospects enjoy a chase
before surrendering to a tempting proposition.

"Follow up ~ follow up ~ follow up!"

Some clients will enthuse at an initial meeting but fail to get back to you when they promised. Always remember, it is your responsibility to win the work not theirs to give it to you ~ as such, if you think the work is there, follow up as many times as necessary until you become certain that the work will not be forthcoming.

"One experienced consultant suggests that many new to the consulting business take a long time to understand the lengthy cycle times between first phone call or meeting and work finally resulting. This can be many weeks, months and sometimes even years. However long it takes, it pays to follow up and keep in touch."

Submit proposals ~ a drag but it pays off

Writing proposals can seem a tedious waste of time but keep at them. Research shows that people who write proposals ~ even when they don't need to ~ get bigger and better assignments. Don't forget, most proposals can be 're-cut' or adjusted in small ways for other future clients if they are well written in the first place.

"A small marketing consultancy maintains all its proposals on a central computer database for everyone to access as they wish. They believe this considerably reduces the need to write proposals from scratch ~ in some cases, with a little 'cut and paste' 90% of even a long proposal may be already written."

The Irresistible Proposal.
Get ready with the champagne, unless you got the recipe wrong,
and the prospect reports back with symptons of indigestion.

Your proposal ~ a multi-function document

If you used to write proposals within an organisation, remember that the objectives for these were usually to inform rather than win business. You'll need to change your style, as your objectives are now very different. In basic terms a proposal needs to offer a specific goal and a clear strategy for getting there under your guidance.

"One corporate executive, turned organisational consultant, always likes to identify the 'value propositions' or what he likes to describe as the 'pay off points' first. By this, he means he likes to list each tangible 'payoff' for the client by adopting his proposed approach and working with him ~ he then writes his proposal by elaborating on these points!"

What to cover in your proposal

There is no single 'format' for a proposal but every proposal needs a short 'executive' summary, a step by step outline of your envisaged approach and a simple summary or conclusion confirming why this approach is the best way forward. Try to write this three stage process in note form on one page before 'fleshing' out your proposal.

"An independent retail marketing consultant developed such an effective proposal template system, she started to sell her proposal templates or checklists commercially. As a result she built not only a useful and profitable sideline business by helping other consultants but also found herself in greater demand, as many of these consultants often asked her to work with them."

Here's a follow-up letter from
the consultant you saw yesterday...

" Thank you for our meeting yesterday.
It was a short meeting, due to your astonishing
ability to home-in on the main issues, or
'cut the crap' as you put it. Your refusal to discuss
my proposal in any detail was a 'master stroke',
and we were spared the futile exercise of exploring
my well-meaning, but ultimately worthless ideas.
I came away from our meeting a much wiser
human being.
                    Yours, etc...

PS I look forward to submitting a revised proposal
6 months from today. This time, I would appreciate
it if you kept your dogs chained."

The follow up letter.
"...a summary of what may have been discussed..."

Send a follow up letter

Every conversation with a prospective client needs a follow-up letter, however short it may be. A follow-up letter should be a simple summary of what may have been discussed or what you would like to suggest to keep things moving.

"One extremely well organised independent management consultant always sends a short one page letter to the client the day after they meet wherever possible. This summarises the discussion briefly and invariably suggests proposed future steps, even if it's just 'I will call again in 6 months time'. They then diary this action so that the follow-up actually happens."

Don't let them forget you

Keep in touch! Call clients or prospects you haven't contacted for, say, six months and ask them how things are and, preferably, pass on some useful information. This isn't a business call as such, but it helps in the process of referrals and business in the longer term. You might like to develop a calendar directory and make sure to call a given prospect on your list every month.

"A small organisation offering psychological consulting services keeps its whole client prospecting list in a computerised sales tracking system. Because it allows them to diary future call-back promises electronically, when they arrive at the office in the morning, the computer will immediately list the client names and phone numbers that need to be called with the notes from the last conversation attached. This low cost software solution is available to anyone who is serious about prospecting."

Use the press.

Announce your presence by firing a shot or two across the bows of the establishment. Choose your target with care!

Use the press ~ be opinionated

Write letters to the trade press, even the national press, expressing an opinion on an item in a recent issue. This keeps your name in front of prospects and clients and underlines your own image. It helps to be a bit controversial, providing you're sure of your ground.

"The managing partner of a large consulting brokerage firm kept writing to one particular monthly journal with thoughts and ideas for future articles and news that might interest their readership. After a few months, he was invited to write a monthly column. Some years later, his column with his picture proudly positioned in the top left corner still appears every month and is read by a large percentage of his target market."

Contribute to journals ~ be a 'gadfly'

Keep your name in front of prospects in your market sector by submitting articles or letters to your trade journals ~ either generating new ideas or relating general issues to the specific interest of your clients and prospects. The more your prospects see your name as a recognised industry figure, the more likely they are to become clients.

"A journalist-turned-consultant retains his old habit of carrying a small spiral bound pad and pen in his pocket at all times. Whenever he hears something new or different, or even an interesting twist on an old idea, he notes it down. He suggests that presentations and Association or Institute network meetings are his favourite places for lots of input. Each month he takes the best two or three of these notes and writes a short informational article about them which he sends off to three or four journals, at least one of which is usually grateful for the copy."

PRESS RELEASE March 23

SMITH'S / BUNGLE BROS
CONSULTANCY COUP

The fledgling Smith's
Consultancy Group
have pleasure in announ-
cing their appointment
as Shake-up Cons-
ultants to the ultra-
stuffy, ultra-prestigious,
ultra-conservative Bungle Bros Toiletries.

Mr Joe Smith and Mr Syd Bungle

The surprise announcement marks the accept-
ance by Bungles of a proposal submitted
by Smiths at a final 'put-up-or-shut-up'
meeting at the Wayside Tavern today.

Joe Smith – the consultants Managing Director
recalls heated discussions between the two
firms at their preliminary meetings.

"But that's all history" says Joe, no more
'bingles' with the Bungles! We are working
together to get Bangle products into
the bonglerooms of every nation on Earth"

The press release.
An opportunity to "crow discreetly"!

Press release:
If it's interesting it can win new business

If you're sending out a press release, include a good photograph as this increases your chances of having the release used. Press releases should not go out too frequently but if you have something new to say three or four times a year this helps to keep your name in the public eye.

"A large consulting firm keeps its press releases to ten lines on a single page at most. These releases are 'stylised' to grab maximum attention and present something new or interesting with an information number to call to obtain a longer descriptive document."

When you win ~
'crow' discreetly and in the right places

Find a way of communicating to your clients your major successes, awards, testimonials, etc. This increases their perception of your value and should lead to increased business. One way to do this without seeming too arrogant is to mix it in with useful information by way of a regular newsletter.

"Another human resource and training consultancy not only actively enters as many of the competitions, schemes and award categories as they can, but sends out a press release when they win, or even just get mentioned when a magazine or journal writes them up(which is regularly). They cut the article or citation out and send it to a group of new prospective companies to publicly demonstrate their expertise."

Come in 17!!
Please proceed to Zone 4 no. 22
We have a client in deep denial!

First report indicates serious weaknesses in
vital functions - major restructure required.
Check:
1. Cash flow needs re-vitalising
2. Staff needs re-training
3. Plant needs replacing
4. Branches need re-locating
5. Ventures need re-financing
6. Creditors need re-assuring
7. Plans need reviewing
8. Aims need re-focussing
9. Energies need re-directing
10. Hope needs re-kindling
Can you attend?

The last recorded exchange with MEC17.
The call came too late, the business collapsed. The little
emergency van and her gallant crew were never seen again.

Be creative ~ don't miss an opportunity to get noticed

In an increasingly competitive world, every consultant needs to aim to stand out from the crowd. The more differently or creatively you can do this, the better, as you don't want to think you are being innovative only to find that everyone is doing something similar.

"A large human resource consultancy developed a leaflet to attach to all of its prospect letters which was designed to look like a tool box. Inside they listed each of the their human resource approaches in the shape of a particular tool and claimed that the client would also have a wide range of tools to us. Most of their clients liked to keep this colourful and eye-catching leaflet pinned to their wall. It was therefore a very prominent advert that won them a lot of on-going work."

Don't wait to be asked

If you spend time travelling on trains or aeroplanes, use the time to scour the trade press for useful articles which could be of benefit to your clients. Send them a photocopy with a hand-written note from you; this keeps you in the front of their minds and reinforces your value to them.

"One management consultant believes that the majority of decision makers in companies often feel under too much pressure to read journals and magazines in any detail. They are therefore grateful when someone does it for them, as long as what you send is relevant to them. He takes care to ensure that it is, and then follows up a few days later to see whether he can arrange a meeting to discuss possible ways in which they might work together ~ all part of developing a relationship."

"...an opportunity to demonstrate your capacity
to lead and co-ordinate.."

Initiate actions rather than follow others

If you find yourself at one of those business 'social' gatherings, 'networking' with a gin and tonic in your hand, you can make the best use of your time by acting as the leader of the network rather than a passive follower. To do this, you need to suggest a subject or a topic about which the group has an interest and offer future opportunities to share information about it. This helps to demonstrate your capacity to lead and co-ordinate in the eyes of those who may want you to do so in their organisation.

"One management consultant likes to go to 'networking' meetings that have a theme or subject in which they have some particular expertise. They prepare their input carefully, even sometimes putting three or four overheads together. When asked for input they can use the overhead projector to show the group the charts or ideas that they 'just happen' to have in their bag!"

It pays to pamper your clients.
Golden eggs are rare, but rewards can come in
unexpected ways.

Your clients are your ambassadors

Clients are a good source of advertising for you through referrals, but you may have to guide them gently towards the best way to achieve professional and effective referrals that are suitable for your particular market area.

"A management consultant involved in a lot of 're-organisation' and 're-engineering' work always likes to ask who he can call upon in his client's supplier organisations or customers. He generally gets a 'warm' introduction with a client's blessing, and almost invariably gets quality time and an open opportunity to make his pitch."

Your best prospect

It's a maxim of marketing that your best prospect is your existing customer, so spend some time every week thinking of ways that you could be of more benefit to your clients and send them a letter or memo to tell them about it.

"A partner in a multi-national consulting firm suggests that they work on the principle that it is four to five times harder to win a new prospect than to win new work from a past or existing client. They therefore make sure that they spend as much as half of their prospecting contact time in their existing client base."

SECTION 2

Charging for your services

Second rate payment = second rate commitment
= second rate outcomes.

"The labourer is worthy of his hire"

Charging for your services is more of an 'art' than a 'science'. Charge too much and you could have no work. Charge too little and your potential clients may assume your skills are not up to standard.

In practice, new players may charge a little less to get started. One approach is to accept an amount that you feel is reasonable in return for your efforts. As you gain experience, you can raise, (or lower), your fees, in accordance with your estimate of time, and costs for each job. Also whether or not the job will lead to additional work.

Of course the clients 'budget', or what they are prepared to pay is a factor. They may pay generously, but if they won't agree to pay your 'reasonable fee', perhaps you don't need their work, especially if there are better customers around the corner, down the track or in the pipeline.

The 'going rate' is an ellusive benchmark.
Perhaps its because everyone works at their own bench.

Your skills are valuable resources ~ user should pay

Don't feel that 'diagnostic help' or needs analysis work should be offered free as a 'sprat to catch a mackerel'. Often, simply identifying the problem is the major part of the solution and could be your most valuable offering.

"One new arrival to management consulting cautioned that they started their business by offering a FREE half day of 'diagnostic' consulting. Whilst the phone didn't exactly run 'hot', over 6 months he was brought in to companies on seven separate occasions. Everyone thanked him but never once offered him paid work. He realised that the companies that would take advantage of his offer typically wouldn't normally use consultants at all ~ he therefore started charging for all of his work."

Establish your fees ~ per day or for specific service at a fixed sum

It's better to quote fixed fees rather than an hourly or daily rate, as clients tend to find this easier to plan for and it has the effect of ensuring that you protect your overall profit margin.

"One experienced consultant suggests that all new consultants should always type up a list of the services they offer and the fees that they would like to earn (that realistically reflect their experience). They should keep this list close at hand to keep reminding themselves to maintain these rate-earning goals as often as possible so as not to erode their value in the market place."

Why is your quote so precise?
There's a better answer than the above.
The paragraph headed 'Quoting a job' may help here.

Keep to a professional level of charges

Provided that your business terms are reasonable and comparable with your competition, stick to your guns. Consultants who are excessively flexible and available rarely get good business.

"A large compensation and benefits consulting firm, experienced in salary survey work, suggests that management consultants are amongst the worst groups of people for claiming to be earning the "going-rate" but then accepting 30%, 40% or even 50% less in reality. This tends to adversely affect the whole consulting market. They advise that the majority of clients know the 'going-rate' and expect to pay it unless the consultants themselves are lacking in confidence to ask for it!"

If the prospect questions your fees

Don't bargain with the client over fees. If they insist on a reduction, reduce the work you do for them. Bargaining makes you a less desirable product or service and often gives the wrong image.

"Large consulting firms often command the highest daily fees and rarely negotiate to reduce their rates. One consultant from such a firm suggests that the only basis upon which to reduce fees is when the client will commit to a long minimum days contract or retainer arrangement. However, he believes that great care is needed even in these circumstances as a client might expect the same rate for 'one-off' short term work in the future."

However ~ having said that, let me say this! ...

Payment terms ~
Should be clearly stated before work is commenced

Make sure your clients know exactly what your terms of business are ~ in recessionary times, clients may assume that 30 days really means 60 or even 90 days! This doesn't always guarantee you'll get paid on time but it can help you to get your invoices paid close to when they should be.

"One independent consultant was experiencing many months of delay in being paid for their work from several clients. He changed his terms from 30 to 14 days and offered a 2% discount for payment before the due date. He claims that over 95% of his invoices are now paid on or before they are due."

Value for service

Your fees should be based on the value of the services provided, not the time expended.

"Many medium and large sized consulting firms now offer to consult at a lower rate (or sometimes for nothing!) in return for a share of the benefits or the 'value' that is added. Whilst they typically say that most clients don't take these offers up, they do expect the value added to exceed the cost of the total cost of hiring the consultant by some margin. Where possible, they therefore identify how much value they believe they will add in their proposals and charge their fees at a significant level below this amount."

Expenses? What Expenses?

Make it clear when you are charging for your time

If you intend to charge for first meetings or pitches with prospects, make sure they are fully aware of this and the fees involved.

"A new consultant 'burned' several first prospects by sending in an invoice for one or two hours at a preliminary discussion meeting. After the second annoyed client called him on the telephone he changed his tactics. Now he offers the first meeting for free but restricts it to no more than an hour."

Fee cutting ~ think again

Don't be tempted to cut your fee because of the 'exposure' you will get or the 'potential' the project offers. 'Potentials' don't pay the bills and you'll get exposure whether you charge a fee or not.

"A management consultant in a financial services firm advises that every consultant should expect their client to ask them to cut or reduce their fees. He suggests that the best response is to stress the value that will be added and the benefits that will accrue if the consultant is not distracted by a rate that is forced to be lower than the 'norm'."

Your expenses are additional to fees

Clients generally prefer you to charge travel and accommodation fees on a day rate rather than individually and this also avoids criticism about how you spend your expenses. You might like to consider having a selection of set rates according to the area ~ i.e. metropolitan rates, rural rates, and even overseas travel rates etc.

"A large financial consulting firm attaches an expenses schedule to all their quotes and proposals for complete clarity. For long distance travel (over 2 hours by car or plane), they even charge travelling time at 50% of their full consulting rate."

Sorry! business is business!
There's a difference between an estimate and a quote.

Costing a job ~ the difference between an 'Estimate' and a 'Quote'

Be extremely careful when you are asked to estimate your consulting costs or to provide a quote. If you provide an estimate, it is a broad prediction and it may vary. However, a quote is almost always seen to be a fixed and binding rate or lump-sum over and above which costs should never run. If they do, it will be your cost and not the clients, unless you have separated some specific costs or expenses from your quote.

"An individual consultant was 'caught' with having to stick with a fixed quote job on their very first assignment. They ended putting in twice the time that they had estimated in their quotation and obviously made no profit on the work."

Quoting a job

Try quoting a non-rounded figure for a given project ~ such as $1,296 rather than $1,300. Although it may appear to be trivial, It makes it seem that you have really thought through your costings and cut out any wastage.

"One very large consulting firm always calculates their 'overhead' contribution at 39.25%. This always creates a very particular unique and non rounded rate or figure that gets quoted to the client."

The consultant's initiation.
It's a significant event when you get your first advance payment.

How to get paid in advance

You can get part of your fee up front if you are prepared to show the necessary confidence in your clients' need to employ you. Ask for the advance then stand eyeball to eyeball with the client and say nothing ~ the first person to speak loses! If the client thinks the job is more important to you than your terms of business, you won't get the advance fee; but if the client thinks that the advance is an essential part of hiring your services, then they'll pay.

"One consulting business specialising in a lot of customer service 'focus group' work and 'mystery' shopping, invariably asks for one third of the overall fee up-front, to cover direct expenses and out-lays that they incur almost immediately in their type of work. They say their clients are typically fairly indifferent about doing this, as long as the majority of the fee is to be paid upon successful completion. This gives them the perceived control over the end result of the work."

What to list in your invoices

Don't clutter your invoice with minor charges for phone calls or bits of photocopying unless these are significant expenses. Add an allowance for these to your normal rate as an overhead cost.

"One information technology firm always lists its major charges in brackets on all of its invoices (even when the charges are zero!). They quote 'charges for phone, fax, typing, desk top publishing, e-mail, postage, handling, collation, stationery, disks, photocopying, binding and administrative co-ordination' ~ pretty much covers all eventualities!"

The attitude of the praise-retentive client.
"Never tell the consultant what a great job
he or she has done, because that's a signal
that says "It's OK to be charged more next time"."

Fee strategies

What? Your fees have gone up again?

You shouldn't raise your fees too often, so raise them by enough to cover yourself for at least nine months, preferably a year.

"One lone consultant, starting out, set their fees far too low at the outset and was faced with have to 'walk up' their fees several times over the ensuing months. Because his clients started to complain, he switched to a competitive day rate instead of hourly rate and promoted that this would be fixed at this level for the next 2 years -the clients welcomed this stability."

A marketable client benefit ~ when about to raise your fees

If you intend to raise your fees, use this occasion to provide a benefit to your existing clients by announcing that you intend to raise your charges from now on, but that they will be continued to be charged at the old rate for three or six months. Alternatively, you could suggest that consulting work committed by them before the date will be charged at the lower rate.

"One large management consulting firm reviews their charged out rates at the beginning of each new fiscal year. Three months before this change, they make sure that they send out a flier which promotes that all consulting contracts signed before this date will be performed on the old rates."

Two consultants meet while escorting their consortia on a discovery tour through the land of better management.

Bargain offers for clients needing identical approaches

If you spend time developing an actual product ~
i.e. something that can easily be used for a number of clients
without the need to be changed, don't charge the full
development costs to the first client who uses it, as this will
make you uncompetitive and possibly unpopular. Spread the
cost on a pro rata basis over the number of clients who you
expect to be able to sell it to over 12–18 months.

*"A very large financial and tax consulting firm often develops
procedure manuals for many of its clients. When a particular piece of
written work can be used again, almost in its entirety, their approach
is to charge 20–25% of the full development cost and then charge 15%
to subsequent clients. This makes the later clients very profitable for
them but also keeps their prices low, which wins them more new
work."*

When the prospect can't afford your services

Don't dismiss clients with small budgets out of hand but try to
encourage them to club together with clients who have similar
needs to buy your services on a consortium basis.

*"An innovative marketing consultancy offered monthly small-
business network meetings, with the express intention of creating a
forum in which common issues and problems could be discussed, and a
potential partner or two found to provide the consulting support.
Much of their research work, in particular, is now often performed for
a small consortia of businesses who spread their costs under this
system."*

The short, cheap "saturation consultation".
Where a hesitant client's resistance is weakened by a concentrated
bombardment of value added possibilities.

A Nominal fee for an initial consultation with non-starters

One way to deal with small clients with low budgets is to charge a nominal fee for initial consultations. That way you don't waste your time on companies who can't really afford you.

"A lone human resource consultant promoted a one hour consultation for a half an hour rate to businesses with less than 25 people. Several organisations took the offer up and the consultant made sure that they identified as many value added issues as possible in the time. Around 1 in 3 of these clients went ahead with further consulting at the full rate."

The client/consultant relationship

Harmony through communication.
In tonights performance, the Consultant conducts his Clients
through the haunting "Management Variation" followed by the
familiar "Franchise" movement from the glorious
Brandenburger Concerto by J. P. Bach.

"Making sweet music together"

It goes without saying that communication between you and your client is one of the most critical factors in your overall success as a consultant. However, the communication often unfolds casually or flows by accident from one phone call or meeting to the next. The trick is to manage the communication process at all times and, at least appear to be in control (in the most friendly, open and co-operative way possible).

Co-operation is always top priority.

A consulting appointment is *not* a grand slam tournament. Achievement shared with a client is better than winning *against* an opponent.

Work with the client ~
co-operation is always the top priority

Don't let your relationship with a client deteriorate in any way, especially if it affects communications. Remember that your role, first and foremost, is to serve the client, so stop doing any work and patch up any problems before continuing or moving on.

"After a particularly loud and angry argument, one consultant deliberately spent the rest of the day working on another floor in the client's building and assumed the problem would 'blow-over'. Not being able to find the consultant to discuss the matter more sensibly the client decided that he would terminate the consultant's contract. This termination hurt both of their pockets and the client's reputation."

Before commencing ~ get a written agreement

Ideally, you should always work with some form of written agreement, so that both parties know exactly what is involved in a particular project. This doesn't need to be a 50-page contract, a simple letter will do. However, you should have a document that explains the position, the expectations and the responsibilities of everyone involved.

"A new-to-the-business consultant drafted a simple 3-page contract and paid a small fee for it to be checked by a legal professional for accuracy and completeness. She now attaches this standard template to her client letters to show that she has a simple set of contract paperwork that is clear but should create no worries for client or consultant."

After reading the first draft of our agreement I must object to item 4 which says..."the consultant agrees to redecorate the company manager's residence." It strikes me that this has no relevance to our immediate business objectives!

OK! We'll delete that - if you agree to taking out item 5, where the company agrees to pay the upkeep and training of the consultant's 2 racing greyhounds!

Striking a business agreement is a two-way thing.

A Proposal is not an Agreement

It's not often advisable to combine a proposal with any form of written agreement. Get the client to accept the proposal, then prepare the agreement or contract, which more formally documents what is involved.

"One small consultant learned the hard way that committing to perform certain tasks in a proposal and then signing at the bottom (and leaving space for the client to sign) was seen as an agreement. This left no room for manoeuvre with one client who accepted the proposal and held the consultant accountable for the written commitments (at the consultant's ultimate cost). This was an experience that they didn't repeat again."

Your clients' responsibilities to you

On a major project, make sure that the written agreement includes something to cover the clients' responsibilities in matters such as workspace, secretarial support, expenses not covered in your fee, prompt payment of invoices and so on.

"One large consulting organisation has a list of 25 'points of note' attached to its proposals to clients. This list covers almost every conceivable item that the client will either provide at their cost or will be charged separately. Although this seems like a lot of points, it saves considerable dispute at a later stage."

Insurance.
Visiting consultants, like postmen, can be mistaken for trespassers.

Always cover yourself fully

Some clients may expect you to have public liability or professional indemnity insurance. Even if not requested, you don't want to be sued for everything when your client decides that implementing your advice has cost them a lot of money. The same applies to insuring yourself and your continued income ~ get insured!

"Many lone operators or small consultants forget to get insurance. Unfortunately, there are lots of 'horror' stories about expensive legal suits being brought or even something as simple as a consultant falling seriously ill for a time-as any experienced consultant will tell you. Insurance is a cheap way to create peace of mind."

Inflation protection ~ for long term contracts

If you sign up for a long term contract, protect yourself by writing in an inflation~beating clause that allows you to maintain your income should the inflation rate rise substantially during the course of the contract.

"Nearly all the major or large consulting firms can employ many people who will have expectations of a pay rise every year. As a result, apart from annual reviews of charge out rates, they also budget rate-escalation charges for any consultant employed for longer than 12 months."

"Intuition" or "ability"?
Intuition is fine, but a work schedule is a good motivator.

Time schedules ~ a discipline to motivate both you and your client

Show an awareness of your clients' needs by providing some form of time schedule for the work you intend to do. This schedule may slip, of course, but at least you have indicated that you understand the clients' pressures and need for timeliness.

"One small consulting firm attaches a project 'gantt' chart to its fortnightly reports on which it plots progress in the 6, 8 or 10 areas or tasks in which it is working ~ this creates the positive sense that the project is always moving forward."

Write contact reports to clarify your aims and procedures

Try to get into the habit of writing Contact Reports after major client meetings, covering the points raised, decisions made, action to be taken and who is responsible. This helps you to plan out your working time if you have several clients, as well as providing your client with a written reference on what you have been briefed to accomplish. It also helps to prevent any subsequent misunderstandings.

"One management consulting firm prints its own contract report booklet in which each consultant is expected to tick boxes and write summary notes after each client meeting. As this sheet is carbonated in triplicate they can also give one to the client, put one on the file and keep one for themselves."

Singin' the "Associate Consultant Blues"!

Call in other help when you need it ~ it's part of your job as a consultant

You can enhance your own credibility by being honest with prospects and recommending other professionals ~ or in-house staff ~ for aspects of a given project rather than yourself. This shows that you put the clients' interests above your own.

"One consultant won considerable regard when she suggested that two or three staff that she had met that were employed by the client would complete a piece of project work more quickly and cost effectively than she might do by herself. She offered to steer the team and transfer some of her skills to them at no extra cost. Far from losing work, she won even more work on different projects in the future."

Calling in other consultants ~ the risks

If you work with subcontractors or associates, make sure you have some form of legal protection that prevents them from setting up on their own and taking your clients with them.

"A young general management consulting firm claimed that it was too busy to set up proper contracts and get people to sign confidentiality agreements. Unfortunately, several of the sub-contract consultants not only copied or adapted their approach but successfully contacted their clients directly and started consulting on their own!"

Make friends with the staff.
A hostile work environment can turn a straight-forward task
into a nightmare obstacle course.

"We don't like outsiders!"

When you're working alongside staff in a client company, you can be perceived as a threat. You can overcome this by making sure that you and your role are properly introduced and explained to members of staff. It's also important to make sure they are aware that you will be working through them, not against them or at their expense.

"One small consulting firm, working with industrial clients, will not take on any consulting assignment until it has 'walked the shop floor' and talked to some of the people that are likely to be affected by the assignment."

When to share or step out of the limelight

Occasionally you may have to swallow your pride and let players in the client company take the credit for your achievements. It's not always easy but it's good for business and the people who really matter will know who's responsible for the success.

"One consultant had spent over 18 months with a client, helping them to achieve a major change initiative. When the senior executive client manager was publicly thanked at a meeting for their 'vision, drive and hard work', the consultant felt extremely deflated. However, after the meeting, the chief executive privately thanked the consultant and suggested that he would like to engage him for a further 6 months to help settle down the change ~ this was a much better reward for all of his efforts."

SECTION 4

Meanwhile, back at the office...

From small acorns, large oaks do grow, if they are well maintained, developed, merged and listed on the stock exchange.

Maintaining and Developing your Consultancy

In the effort to keep prospecting, performing assignments and keeping the cash flowing, it is important to remember that your consulting business needs a little administrative "oiling" from time to time.

This means *reviewing*. Reviewing what you've done successfully (making sure that you keep up the good work), and reviewing the work that you feel could have been better, in order to adjust and improve in the future.

Oh NO!
Opportunity knocked, but the bell tolled, the horse bolted, the stable door was left to gather moss, and the answering machine is demanding an apology!

"I'm returning your call"

Telephone messages should be responded to the same day, or at the latest, by the next day without fail.

"Every consultant fears the missed call that loses them business ~ one consultant forgot to call a client back for over a week and lost a large contract that should have started immediately ~ a hard way to learn the lesson!"

"Thanks for your interest" ~ acknowledge all correspondence

You should always reply to letters as soon as you can and certainly within a week. Even if you need more time to submit a full answer, send a letter to acknowledge receipt and give a projected date for the full reply.

"One experienced consultant suggests that many clients are very slow to put pen to paper and keep you informed. However, this doesn't make them any more tolerant or patient regarding information from the consultant when they want it. As a result, respond as quickly as you can, it is in your interests."

Subcontracting and joint projects

Don't treat your competitors purely as rivals, you can get a lot of business by subcontracting some of their work or by working on joint projects. Let them know you're available for non-conflicting subcontracting or mutual arrangements.

"Several small consultants regularly claim that a co-operative agreement with like-minded consultants can help to smooth the peaks and troughs of consulting work ~ look for three or four consulting firms that would compliment your work and discuss how you might work together from time to time."

Opportunity knocks again...
in the form of a subcontract!

When to bring in outside help

If you've got so much work on that you haven't got time to do your own marketing, it might be worth taking on a professional marketer or subcontracting some of your lower level work so that you can better service your clients.

"One very busy management consultant decided to hire a junior consultant over 4 days a week. Although she was concerned that this would eat her profit margin entirely, in actual fact, it added 60% to her overall income and allowed her to do a lot more of the work that interested her most."

Building a reserve fund

Every time you receive a payment, put 10% into a building society or other interest-bearing account and forget it. This will give you a handsome supplement to your pension arrangement if things go well or emergencies fund if things go really badly in the future.

"In the early days of consulting you may feel you need all of your consulting fees to earn a living. However, one consultant who saved nothing for 8 years, started adopting the 10% saving system and was amazed how this discipline quickly built his retirement fund ~ he only wished he had done this from the outset."

The Ultimate Consultant.
Few of us can hope to reach this level of skill.
Here, the legendary Hank Springer reveals a sensitivity which took
him to the pinnacle of his profession.

Update and recycle the good stuff ~
improve the less successful

Not all your proposals will win the business, so review, remodel and recycle them for other prospects. If you keep retaining your best work in your new proposals, your continuous improvement approach will win you new work.

"As your experience as a consultant builds, you will begin to be able to separate your excellent or outstanding work from work that meets a need but perhaps does not have that same edge. One very experienced consultant suggests that it is worth keeping the 'highly outstanding work' and looking to use it again in other companies where this is possible. He claims that the same basic piece of work can be used 10, 15 or even 20 times in slightly modified form over several years with different clients."

Take time for research ~
it keeps you on your toes at the 'leading edge'

It's worth spending a little time every year simply wandering around a good college or university reference library and browsing through the papers and articles relevant to your sphere of operation. It stimulates your thought processes and may trigger new ideas for you to offer or new client opportunities.

"One small consultant has developed an excellent long term relationship with their local university librarian. By cultivating the professional relationship and explaining what they do the librarian keeps an eye out for interesting books and articles and either puts them aside or keeps a note. When the consultant makes his monthly visit, he has several interesting resources that can often quickly turn to opportunities."

Consultant Dependency.
This is a distressing client condition and
should not be encouraged. Take your holiday and send your
client to a support group.

Ongoing development of your consultancy

Review what seem to be the common needs of past and present clients and learn from this to develop new services which you should be providing and how much you should be charging for them.

"A highly successful consultant, who has been consulting for over 20 years, suggests that it is valuable to look at the 'mix' of consulting services you provide over a two to three year period and to ask the question 'is this the mix I was looking for or one that evolved from an enjoyment/financial perspective?' If it is the latter you can actively change your marketing strategy in the future."

Take time out to regularly enjoy other facets of your life

Build a time for positive relaxation into your schedule. Relaxation doesn't just mean doing nothing, but is most effective when your energies are devoted to something you enjoy doing for its own sake. Leave your office, lock the door and have fun!

"A large consultancy is widely known for its 14 to 15 hour consulting days, serious dedication and unrelenting focus on outputs and results. However, every quarter, to ensure that at least some fun creeps into proceedings, Friday afternoon is entirely given over to having fun with a range of sporting activities and games. The employees love the change and are refreshed. They talk about the events for weeks afterwards."

Summary

This small book has offered some simple tips and real examples for the experienced or inexperienced consultant to adopt in the right place and at the right time. We don't claim that every tip or idea will always work or always fit in every situation. However, we do believe that consultants who think carefully about the service they are offering, and are able to offer a few 'different' ideas to the market, will inevitably stand out and succeed. Keep in mind, clients hire you to get access to your unique skills and knowledge.

As you gain more experience, you add to your skills and business contacts. This in turn, tends to bring in more work, until eventually, you get to choose only those assignments you know are likely to be the most rewarding, creatively or financially.

At the same time, your own consultancy business will showcase your marketing ability. You will have built a consultancy which has become a valuable resource for management. One with a reputation of accomplishment and reliability.

ACKNOWLEDGEMENTS

This book would not have been possible without the input and suggestions from literally hundreds of people far too numerous to mention individually. However, substantial contributions were made by several consulting organisations and client organisations and they are listed below:

- Andersen Consulting
- Arthur Andersen
- Barker and Wallis Consulting Group
- Boston Consulting Group
- Carlson Marketing
- Change Alliance
- Coopers and Lybrand
- C R Group
- Creative Learning Concepts
- Cressap
- Cull Egan and Dell
- Drake Consulting
- E M D
- Ernst and Young
- Focal Point
- Hampshire International
- Management Learning Resources
- Mercer International
- Mitchell Consulting
- Morgan and Banks
- R T O Consultants
- Pears Consulting
- Polson Training and Consulting
- Price Waterhouse
- Roevin Consulting
- S M S
- Synergy Consulting Group
- Training Solutions Group
- Wilson Learning
- Wise Solutions

Warm thanks are offered to every one of these organisations and everyone else who contributed. Of course, we are more than happy to hear about other tips and anecdotes from any consulting firm in the world!